Textbook 4

Herausgegeben von
Gisela Ehlers

Erarbeitet von
Gisela Ehlers, Ursula Michailow-Drews, Hannelore Tait, Michaela Schönau, Anna Van Montagu und Anne Zeich-Pelsis

Auf der Grundlage von
Bumblebee Textbook 4 (2013/2014) von
Gisela Ehlers, Grit Kahstein,
Matthias Muth, Hannelore Tait und Christina Meindl

Muttersprachliche Beratung
Elspeth Corrie

Illustriert von
Juliane Assies, Heike Heimrich,
Elisabeth Holzhausen, Oda Ruthe,
Friederike Schumann und Ulrike Vetter

Schroedel
westermann

Contents

Hello again   3
- What do you remember?

Back to school   4–7
- Subjects
- Timetable
- Because

Golden Time   8–13
- Activities at Golden Time
- What are you planning to do tonight?
- Sherlock Holmes
- Treasure Island

At home   14–19
- Furniture
- Rooms
- Story: Mum's house, Dad's flat

At work   20–25
- Jobs
- Job descriptions
- What do you want to be?
- Butler / Captain

At the zoo   26–31
- Zoo animals
- What animals like
- Vet / Zookeeper

Earth day   32–37
- In the park
- Save nature: Collecting waste
- Oceans in danger
- Song: With my own two hands

Children of the world   38–43
- People in Great Britain
- Pen pals
- A video call with a pen pal

Holidays   44–51
- Holiday locations / Activities
- Holiday plans
- Rap: Coconut cream rap
- Buying tickets
- The Highland games / Dance: Boston Tea Party

All through the year   52–57
- Guy Fawkes Day
- Thanksgiving
- St Patrick's Day

The story of the leprechaun   58–59

Fit for five   60–63

Look it up   64–74
- How to ... 64–67
- Work together 68–69
- Look it up 70–79

Impressum 80

▶ Ich kann von meinen Sommerferien erzählen.

Hello again

Fantastic holiday!

Relax in Hyde Park.

Fun with Mum and Dad.

At a petting farm.

Yummi!

What did you do in your summer holiday?

I went to Italy.
I liked spaghetti very much.

I stayed at home.
I went to London Eye.
One day I went swimming.

1 Talk about the pictures.

2 Listen to the children and read along.

3 Talk about your holiday.

4 Make a mindmap.

Von den Sommerferien erzählen.
Diff ▲ KV 92

- How to S. 65
- CD 1
- KV 92

three 3

Back to school

	Monday	Tuesday	Wednesday	Thursday	Friday
9.00 – 9.15	Assembly	Assembly	Assembly	Assembly	Assembly
9.15 – 10.15	Maths	Maths	Maths	Maths	Maths
10.15 – 10.30	Break	Break	Break	Break	Break
10.30 – 11.30	English	English	English	English	English
11.30 – 12.30	ICT	German	Music	Art	ICT
12.30 – 1.30	School dinner	School dinner	School dinner	School dinner	School dinner
1.30 – 2.30	Science	Science	Project	ICT	German
2.30 – 3.30	Crafts	PE	Project	PE	Golden Time

When do we have PE?

Who is our new music teacher?

1 Listen and point.
2 Name the subjects.
3 Act out the dialogue.
4 Talk about your timetable.

four

Schulfächer benennen können und Zeitangaben machen.
Diff ▲ KV 4
Wdh: Activities at school

- FC/WC 1–13, WB S. 4–6
- CD 2/3
- KV 1/2/4

▶ Ich kann über meinen Stundenplan sprechen.

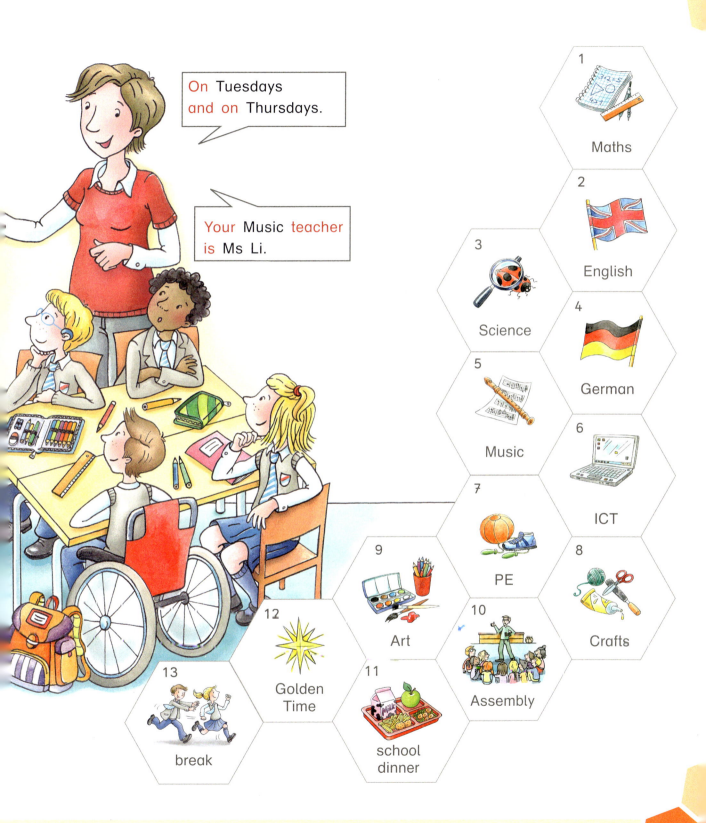

What have the children got on Mondays/...?
How long is a lesson?
How long is a school day?

When is the first break?
What subjects are different from German schools?

five

▶ Ich kann etwas über englische Schulfächer erzählen.

Lisa's letter: Subjects

 It's English now, speak, speak, speak!

Now it's Art, draw, draw, draw!

Then it's Maths, count, count, count!

Music next, sing, sing, sing!

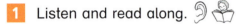 It's German now, read, read, read!

Golden Time, fun, fun, fun!

1 Listen and read along.

2 Do the rap.

Hallo Leute,
die Schule hat wieder angefangen und wir haben unseren neuen Stundenplan bekommen. Da gibt es zum Beispiel das Fach *ICT*. Das steht für *Information and Communication Technology*. Hier lernen wir, am Computer zu arbeiten. Das macht Spaß. Das Fach *Science* ist auch sehr interessant. Wir lernen eine Menge über Pflanzen und Tiere, machen Experimente und erfahren viel über die Geschichte Großbritanniens. Wenn wir *Golden Time* haben, können wir uns aussuchen, was wir am liebsten machen möchten. Ich hole mir dann gern Bücher aus unserer Bücherei (*library*). In *PE, Physical Education*, spielen wir oft Mannschaftsspiele.

Love Lisa

3 Read Lisa's letter. Talk about it.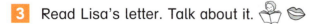

4 Find more information about British schools.

▶ Ich kann begründen, warum ich etwas mag oder nicht mag.

Let's talk: What I like about school

What subjects do you like?

I like Music because I like singing.

What subjects don't you like?

I don't like Art because I don't like drawing.

I like ...	Music Maths German English	because I like ...	speaking. drawing. reading. singing.
I don't like ...	PE Art Crafts Science	because I don't like ...	learning about nature. counting. working with computers. playing ball games.

1 Listen and read along.

2 Practise the dialogue.

3 Write your own list: I like .../I don't like ...

Sätze mit *because* verbinden.
Diff ▲ KV 6/7, Diff ▼ KV 8/10

• FC/WC 1–9/12
• CD 7
• KV 6–8/10

Golden Time

1 Listen and point.

2 Talk about the picture.

3 Talk: What would you like to borrow?

In einer Bücherei ein Buch ausleihen.
Diff ▲ KV 23/24

▶ Ich kann erzählen, was britische Kinder während einer Freiarbeitsstunde machen.

What can you see?
What can you read on the poster?
What time is it?
What's your favourite book/computer game?
What is not allowed in the media room?
What would you like to do during Golden Time?

▶ Ich kann andere fragen, was sie vorhaben, und auf diese Frage antworten.

Let's talk: What are you planning to do?

listen to a CD · work with a tablet · read a book · play computer games · draw

What are you planning to do?

I want to read a book. And you?

I want to play a computer game.

I'm planning to watch a programme on Sherlock Holmes.

1 Listen to the dialogue and read along.

2 Practise the dialogue.

3 Act it out.

▶ Ich kann etwas über Sherlock Holmes erzählen.

Lisa's letter: Sherlock Holmes

Hi Leute,
meine Oma ist gerade aus Deutschland zu Besuch. Sie liebt Krimis, besonders die Geschichten über den Detektiv Sherlock Holmes, der Verbrechen durch logisches Denken und einen scharfen Verstand aufklärt. Sherlock Holmes hat es nie wirklich gegeben, der Autor Sir Conan Doyle hat ihn sich ausgedacht. Trotzdem gibt es hier in London das Sherlock Holmes Museum in der Baker Street 221b. Hier kann man das angebliche Wohn- und Arbeitszimmer von Sherlock ansehen. Also ein Zimmer einer Person, die es nie gab. Meine Oma und ich hatten trotzdem Spaß. Vielleicht werde ich mir demnächst einige der Geschichten aus der Schulbücherei holen.

Eure Lisa

1 Read Lisa's letter.
2 Find more information about the museum.
3 Do you know more detective stories?

▶ Ich kann diese Geschichte vorlesen.

Treasure Island

Jim finds a treasure map. He and his friends want to find the treasure.

They sail to Treasure Island with John Silver and his crew. One night, Jim finds out that they are pirates.

On the island Jim meets Ben Gunn. He knows where the treasure is.

John Silver and his pirates look for the treasure but can't find it.

There is a big fight.

Jim and his friends escape with the treasure and sail home. And John Silver?

1 Listen and read along.

2 Read it out loud.

3 Talk about your favourite stories.

▶ Ich kann den Weg zum Schatz beschreiben.

The treasure hunt

land at … beach

walk through the forest

swim through the river

walk into the cave

dive under the waterfall

walk around the lake

climb the rock

walk over the rope bridge

1 Listen and find the treasure.

2 Hide a treasure. Tell your partner the way.

At home

1. Listen, read and speak along.
2. Talk about the picture.

▶ Ich kann Räume und Möbel benennen.

What can you see on the poster?
Where do you live? In a flat or a house?
How many rooms have you got?

What is in the children's bedroom?
What is in your bedroom?

fifteen

▶ Ich kann über mein Wunschzimmer sprechen.

Let's talk: My dream room

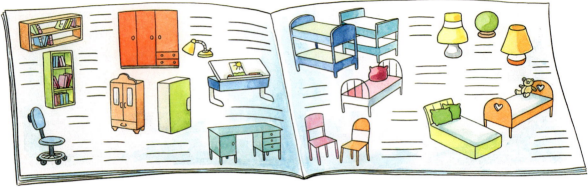

What would you like to have in your room?

I'd like to have a big sofa.

Why?

Because I like to read a lot of books.

1 Listen to the dialogue.

2 Practise the dialogue.

▶ Ich kann ein Gedicht lesen.

I love my home

I live in a flat
high up there.
Where the sun shines in,
up in the air.

There are lifts and stairs,
and ten floors.
There are balconies too,
and windows and doors.

Our flat is just right,
not too big, not too small.
We have got four rooms
plus a kitchen and hall.

I like to live here.
It really is fun.
I am very near
to the moon and the sun!

Hallo Ihr in Deutschland,
mir ist aufgefallen, dass viele Häuser in Großbritannien
mindestens einen Schornstein, einen *chimney*, haben. Grund dafür ist,
dass es in vielen der Wohnzimmer einen Kamin, den sogenannten
fireplace gibt.
Auf diesen gemütlichen Platz möchte hier niemand verzichten.
In Städten sind die Kamine nur Nachbildungen, weil es sonst zu viel
Luftverschmutzung (*smog*) geben würde. In diesen Nachbildungen
darf kein echtes Feuer brennen, sondern nur ein
electric fire, wie Ihr es auf dem Bild sehen könnt.

Eure kuschelig warme
Lisa

1 Read the poem. Learn it by heart.
2 Read Lisa's letter. Compare to your countries.

Mum's house, Dad's flat

▸ Ich kann eine englische Geschichte mitlesen.

1. Listen to the story and read along.
2. What has Cathy got at her Mum's house / her Dad's flat?
3. What does she do at her Mum's house / her Dad's flat?

At work

1. Listen to the presentation.
2. Talk about the jobs.
3. Describe the uniforms.

▶ Ich kann einige Berufe benennen.

Who wears a uniform at work?
Which jobs are presented?
What's your favourite job?

What would you like to know about the jobs?

▶ Ich kann Berufsbeschreibungen verstehen.

Lots of jobs

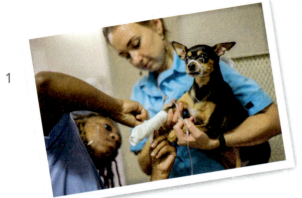

Interview 1:
Miss Spencer is 34 years old.
She works in our area.
She loves her job
because she helps people in danger.
If you need help, call 9-9-9. Who is it?

Interview 2:
Mr Batson is 58 years old.
His job is very interesting
because he meets many
people when he brings
postcards, letters or parcels.
Who is it?

Interview 3:
Ms Johnson works in her
practice at 4 Oxford Road.
She likes her job because she
wants to help sick animals.
Her patients are hamsters,
guinea pigs, cats, dogs, birds
and many more. Who is it?

1 Read Lisa's notebook.
2 Guess the jobs.
3 Listen to the interviews and check.
4 Describe the last photo.

twenty-two

Unbekannten Lesetexten Informationen entnehmen.
Diff ▲ KV 46/48, Diff ▼ KV 43/45

- FC/WC 44/46/50/52, WB S. 16
- CD 26
- KV 43/45/46/48

▶ Ich kann andere fragen, was sie werden wollen, und die Frage beantworten.

Let's talk: When I grow up

postman

football player

waiter

kindergarten teacher

bodyguard

butler

What do you want to be when you grow up?

I want to be a pilot because I like to fly.

When I grow up I want to be a police woman.

1 Listen and point.

2 Listen and read along.

3 Practise the dialogue.

Über Berufswünsche sprechen; Sätze mit *because* verbinden.
Diff ▲ KV 42, Diff ▼ KV 41
Wdh: Hobbies, activities

• FC/WC 39–57, WB S. 18
• CD 28
• KV 41/42

▶ Ich kann etwas über Butler erzählen.

Lisa's letter: A butler's work

Hi guys,

Jeff Millers Vater ist Butler. Es gibt eine richtige Schule, um Butler auf ihren Beruf vorzubereiten. Unterrichtsfächer sind z. B. Kleider- und Schuhpflege, Servieren und Silberputzen. Mr Millers Arbeitskleidung ist ein dunkler Anzug mit Weste, weißem Hemd und Krawatte. Als er erzählte, dass er morgens die Zeitung bügelt, damit sein Arbeitgeber keine Druckerschwärze an die Hände bekommt, mussten wir alle sehr lachen. Das wäre kein Job für mich, ich putze nicht gerne. Ich möchte lieber Pilotin werden, wie Marys Mutter. Was wollt Ihr denn so werden?

Eure Lisa

1. Read Lisa's letter.
2. Talk about it. Compare to your countries.

▶ Ich kann verstehen, was ein Schiffskapitän erzählt.

Ahoy!

Hi children.
My name is Captain Meyers.
I work on a big cruise ship.

My ship is 345 m long.
There is a cinema
on my ship
and a theatre.

On my ship there are 1,300 cabins
and 3,000 telephones.
There is room for nearly 2,500 passengers.

For so many people we need lots of things.
We need 490 rolls of
toilet paper every day.
We need 34,000 eggs
every week.

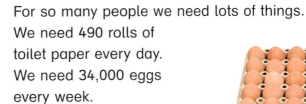

I love my job because I like big ships
and I like meeting new people.

1 Read the text.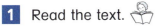

2 Talk about the text in German.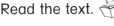

At the zoo

1. Listen and point.
2. Talk about the picture.
3. Plan your day at the zoo.

▶ Ich kann Zootiere benennen.

13 camel
12 tiger
11 parrot
10 penguin
9 lion
8 crocodile
7 chimpanzee
6 zebra
5 giraffe
4 elephant
3 rhino
2 hippo
1 polar bear

Please do not feed the animals.

How many zebras/... can you see?
Which animals would you like to see? Why?
Can you feed the animals?

What do the guinea pigs and rabbits eat?
When do the monkeys/... get their food?
What is Lisa wearing?

twenty-seven

▶ Ich kann Fragen zu Tieren stellen.

Let's talk: New at the zoo

Penguin
Name: Peggy
Habitat: Antarctic
Food: Fish
Age: 3 months

Chimpanzee
Name: Charlie
Habitat: Jungle
Food: Bananas
Age: 8 months

Parrot
Name: Polly
Habitat: Rainforest
Food: Fruit
Age: 2 months

Camel
Name: Carl
Habitat: Desert
Food: Fruit/grass
Age: 10 months

This is Charlie.
He is a chimpanzee.

Chimpanzees live in the jungle.

He eats bananas.

He's 8 months old.

Yes, he can.

Where do chimpanzees live?

What does Charlie eat?

How old is Charlie?

Can Charlie climb?

1 Listen to the keeper's talk and read along.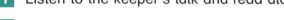

2 Talk about the other animals.

3 Practise the dialogue.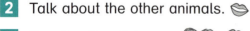

▶ Ich kann etwas über den Londoner Zoo erzählen.

Lisa's letter: At the zoo

Hallo Leute,
den Londoner Zoo gibt es seit 1828. Er ist riesig! Man kann dort über 700 verschiedene Tierarten sehen. Ein Tag reicht dafür gar nicht aus. Am besten gefallen mir die Tierfütterungen, weil die Tierpfleger (zookeeper) dabei Interessantes über die Tiere erzählen und viele Fragen beantworten. Es gibt da ein tolles Angebot, bei dem man einen Tag lang als Hilfstierpfleger (keeper for a day) im Zoo mitarbeiten darf. Emma, Ben und ich werden uns gleich für einen der nächsten Ferientage anmelden! Gibt es sowas bei Euch auch?

Eure Lisa

Teacher's taking us ...

... to the zoo tomorrow ...

1 Talk about Lisa's letter.

2 Listen and sing the song.

▶ Ich kann einen Text über einen Tierarzt verstehen.

Jobs at a zoo: Working as a vet

Hello, my name is Robert Miller.
I am 48 years old and
I work as a vet at the zoo.
Being a vet is my dream job.

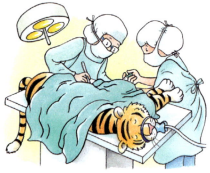

Here you can see me
and my assistant.
We have to operate on
our tiger Peggy.

Sometimes we also have
to measure and weigh our
animals.
This is our tortoise Willy.
Willy is 100 years old.
He is 80 cm tall
and weighs about 200 kg.

Every year we have a lot of
newborn animals at the zoo.
On this photo you can see me
and my assistant with our
baby chimpanzee Tara.

1 Listen and read along.

2 Talk about the text in German.

Einem unbekannten Lesetext Informationen entnehmen;
Sprachmittlung üben.
Diff ▼ Nur mit CD-Track 39 arbeiten.

• CD 39

▶ Ich kann ein Interview mit einem Tierpfleger verstehen.

Jobs at the zoo: Interview with zookeeper Pete

Lisa: What do you need to be a good zookeeper?

Pete: A zookeeper has to love animals. All animals, not just the cool ones. This is most important.

Lisa: Can you tell me more about your job? What are you doing all day?

Pete: Well, I'm not playing with animals all day and making friends with penguins. Being a zookeeper is about looking after animals. I have to prepare their food, clean their cages and look after sick animals. Sometimes I have to call a vet to help me. And don't forget, I also have to talk to the visitors and answer their questions.

Lisa: What is the best part of your job?

Pete: Sometimes a zookeeper has to become a mother of a little baby animal. I love to care for little animals, give them milk and help them survive.

1 Listen, point and read along.   **3** Do a role-play.

2 Talk about the text in German.

Earth day

1. Listen and point.
2. Talk about the picture.
3. Do a role play.

▶ Ich kann Dinge im Park benennen.

What are the children doing?
How many animals can you see?
How many bottles can you see?

Where is the hedgehog/squirrel …?
Can you find the two girl scouts?

thirty-three

▶ Ich kann über Mülltrennung reden.

Let's talk: Helping the earth

battery

Where do the wrappings go?

The wrappings go into the plastic bag.

wrapping

broken glass

The newspaper goes into the paper bag.

comics

Where does the newspaper go?

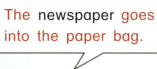
newspaper

empty bottles

can

1 Listen to the dialogue.
2 Practise the dialogue.

▶ Ich kann eine Präsentation verstehen.

Oceans in danger

1. Listen and read along.
2. Listen again and take notes.

▶ Ich kann etwas über britische Läden erzählen.

Lisa's letter: Charity shops

Hi guys,

ich komme gerade vom Einkaufen in einem *charity shop*. Dort hab ich mir Lesestoff gekauft – eine ganze Tüte voll! Da staunt Ihr wohl, wie ich das mit meinem Taschengeld schaffe? In den *charity shops* werden nämlich Bücher, Kleidung und alle möglichen Sachen für ganz wenig Geld verkauft. Diese Sachen haben Leute dem Laden geschenkt, weil sie sie nicht einfach wegwerfen wollen. Der Gewinn geht an eine gute Sache, zum Beispiel an Organisationen, die gegen Krebs kämpfen oder die sich für Kinderprojekte einsetzen. So habe ich schöne Bücher billig bekommen und noch etwas Gutes getan! Übrigens hab ich dort eine Vase wieder gesehen, die wir beim Parkputzen gefunden haben. Klasse, was?

Bis bald,
Lisa

1 Read Lisa's letter. Talk about it.

2 Compare to your countries.

Landeskundliche Informationen über *Charity shops* erhalten.

▶ Ich kann einen Song verstehen.

Song: With my own two hands

I can change the world, with my own two hands.
Make a better place, with my own two hands.
Make a kinder place, oh with my,
oh with my own two hands.
With my own, with my own two hands.
With my own, with my own two hands.

I can make peace on earth, with my own two hands.
And I can clean up the earth, oh with my own two hands.
And I can reach out to you, with my own two hands.
With my own, with my own two hands.
Oh, with my own, oh with my own two hands.

I'm gonna make it a brighter place, (With my own)
I'm gonna make it a safer place, (With my own)
I'm gonna help the human race, (With my own)
(With my own two hands).

Lyrics: Ben C. Harper

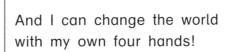

And I can change the world with my own four hands!

1 Listen to the song.
2 Listen and read along.
3 What else did you understand? Talk in German.

Einen unbekannten Songtext verstehen.
• WB S. 26/27
• CD 47
• KV 73

thirty-seven 37

Children of the world

Hi, I'm Matthew. I live in Canada. I like skiing.

Hi, I'm Maureen. I'm 10 years old.

Hi, I'm Samuel. I'm from New York. My city is famous for skyscrapers.

Hello, I'm Gemma. When I grow up I want to work with elephants.

1 Listen and read along.
2 Listen and find out more about the children.
3 Find more English speaking countries.

▶ Ich kann verstehen, was die Kinder über sich erzählen.

Where do the children come from?
What are their hobbies?
Can you describe the flags?

What language do the children speak?
Where would you like to live? Why?

▶ Ich kann etwas über Essgewohnheiten in Großbritannien erzählen.

Lisa's letter: Curry, the new national dish

Hi Ihr in Deutschland,

bei mir an der Schule findet diese Woche eine *International-Food*-Kampagne statt. London ist eine echte Multikultistadt, in der Menschen aus rund 200 Nationen leben. Viele der *foreign born residents*, wie sie hier genannt werden, kommen zum Beispiel aus der Karibik, Afrika oder Indien.
Wir hatten die Aufgabe, ausländische Rezepte zu suchen, die dann in der Schulküche umgesetzt wurden. Meine Klasse hat sich für das neue „englische Nationalgericht" entschieden: ein indisches Curry.
Ravis Vater hat uns gezeigt, wie man das ganz original kocht.
Yummi, das war mal was anderes! Ich bin gespannt, was es morgen gibt.
Bis bald!

Eure Lisa

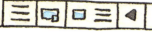 Read Lisa's letter. Talk about it.

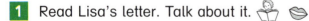 Find out more about "typical" British food.

40 forty   Gesellschaftliche Informationen über Großbritannien erhalten.

▶ Ich kann etwas über die *Flying Doctors* erzählen.

A letter from Amy

Hello England,

I am Amy from Adelaide/Australia.
My hobbies are swimming and reading
and I'm a member of a boomerang club.
When I grow up I want to be a flying doctor. Flying doctors are
important because a lot of people live on farms in the outbacks, far
away from cities and hospitals. So the doctor has to come to them
when they are ill. To become a flying doctor you have to learn to fly
a small plane. I think this is a fascinating job!
I'm also interested in other countries and cultures. Perhaps you would
like to write back and tell me about your home country?

Amy

1 Read Amy's letter. Talk about it.

2 Find out more about the flying doctors.

A letter from Gemma

Hi, I'm Gemma from South Africa.
I live with my parents in a lodge at the Krüger National Park. My Dad is a Park ranger. Visitors come to see and take ~~fotos~~ photos of the Big Five – lion, elephant, buffalo, rhino and leopard. They must stay in their cars and keep doors and windows closed because the animals are wild and dangerous. When I grow up, I want to be a park ranger too. I like the outdoor life and want to show our visitors the beauty of the African bush. If you want to know more about me and my life please, write back to me.
Greetings from South Africa
Gemma

1. Read Gemma's letter. Talk about it.
2. Find out more about the Kruger National Park.

Einen Brief verstehen.
Diff ▾ Mit CD-Track 52 arbeiten.
• CD 52

▶ Ich kann einen Videoanruf verstehen.

Let's talk: A video call with a pen pal

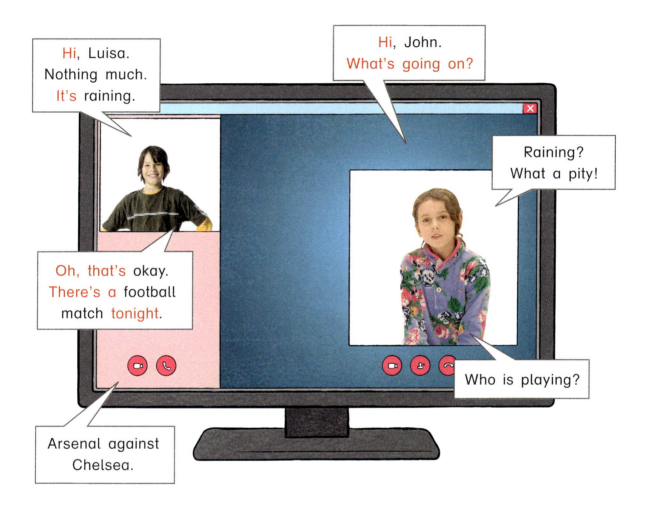

1. Listen and read along.
2. Practise the dialogue.
3. Do a role-play.

Holidays

We're going on a camping trip.

I'm going to Scotland to visit my uncle.

I'm going to stay at home.

1 Listen and read along.
2 Talk about the picture.
3 Talk about your holiday plans.

▶ Ich kann andere zu ihren Ferien befragen.

Let's talk: Going on holiday

	Where?		How?		What?
⚀	mountains		motorbike		go hiking
⚁	sea		car		go snorkelling
⚂	city		plane		visit an old castle
⚃	lake		ferry		go horse-riding
⚄	river		train		go fishing
⚅	stay at home		bus		visit a museum

Where are you going in your holidays?

How will you get there?

I'm going to the seaside.

By train.

What do you want to do there?

I want to go swimming.

1 Listen and point.
2 Practise the dialogue.
3 Play the game.
4 Think of more activites.

46 forty-six

Sich über Ferienpläne unterhalten.
Wdh: Hobbies, activities, sports

• FC/WC 87–104, WB S. 33
• CD 58/59
• KV 84

▶ Ich kann einen Sommersong singen.

Coconut Cream Rap

Text nach Frank Leto

Cream your hands – I cream my hands,
cream your elbows – I cream my elbows,
cream your arms – I cream my arms,
with coconut cream – with coconut cream.

Cream your face – I cream my face,
cream your neck – I cream my neck,
cream your shoulders – I cream my shoulders,
with coconut cream – with coconut cream.

Protect my eyes with glasses, protect my head with a hat,
and when I want to protect my skin – I cream my body with coconut cream.

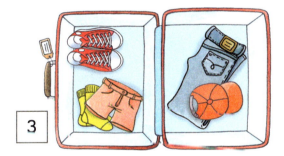

1 Sing the song.

2 Read and choose the right suitcase.

3 Guessing game: Describe another suitcase.

4 Write a list for your trip.

> Ich kann etwas über Ferien in Großbritannien sagen.

Summer holidays

Hallo Ihr alle,
dieses Jahr sind wir während der Ferien zuhause geblieben.
Wir machen zusammen mit meiner Oma tolle Ausflüge, z. B. in den Hyde Park oder nach Windsor Castle, wo die *Royal Family* häufiger ist.
Das Schloss kann man mit dem Boot auf der Themse erreichen.
Ben verbringt die Ferien auf einem Campingplatz am Meer in Südengland.
Emma ist mit ihrer Familie nach Schottland gefahren.
Die Hauptstadt von Schottland ist Edinburgh. Dort gibt es ein großes Schloss (*castle*). Sie wollen zum Loch Ness fahren und Nessie suchen. Glaubt Ihr, dass es Nessie wirklich gibt?
Übrigens tragen in Schottland bei Festen auch Männer Röcke.
Die nennt man *kilts*. Besonders lustig sind auch die Dudelsackspieler.
Der Dudelsack (*bagpipes*) ist ganz schön schwierig zu spielen.
Im September finden hier ganz besondere Sportwettkämpfe statt, die *Highland Games*. Kugelstoßen ist eine Disziplin.
Man nennt das *putting the stone*.

Viele Grüße,
Lisa

1 Read Lisa's letter. What are you doing in your holidays?

Landeskundliche Informationen über Ferien in Großbritannien erhalten.

▶ Ich kann Eintrittskarten kaufen.

A day in Windsor Castle

Tickets for 2 adults and 2 children, please.

Can I help you?

Open
Tuesday – Sunday 9 a.m. – 5 p.m.

Ticket Prices
Adult – £ 12
Group (10 or more) – £ 8 p.p.
Child – £ 6
Children's group – £ 4 p.p.
Family: 2 adults & 3 children – £ 30
Disabled: free entry

1 Listen. What is the text about?

2 Read the information on the notice board. Explain it in German.

3 Practise the dialogues.

▶ Ich kann eine Geschichte über Nessie verstehen.

The Highland Games

Emma and Chris visit the Highland Games. Nessie, the Loch Ness monster, is there, too.

The first game of the day is the piping.

Then they dance a Highland dance.

The next game is putting the stone.

Tossing the caber is the last game.

In the end Nessie wins. She is very proud. Emma and her brother Chris are happy for Nessie.

1. Listen to the story and read along.
2. Find out more about the Loch Ness monster and the Highland Games.

fifty

Eine Geschichte lesen.
Diff ▲ KV 86/100, Diff ▼ KV 88

- SC 17–22
- CD 65
- KV 86/88/100

▶ Ich kann einen schottischen Tanz tanzen.

A Scottish Ceilidh: Boston Tea Party

Stand in 2 lines.

Dance along the lines.

Make a gate and let the next pair dance through it.

Dance through the next gate.

Everyone dance through the gate.

Get back to your position.

1 Get in groups and dance the Ceilidh.
2 Look on the Internet for a video of the dance.

Einen traditionellen Tanz kennenlernen. • CD 67

▶ Ich kann etwas über den Ursprung des Guy Fawkes Day erzählen.

Guy Fawkes Day

Guy Fawkes

On the 5th of November 1605 Guy Fawkes wanted to blow up the Houses of Parliament. He wanted to kill King James 1.

King James

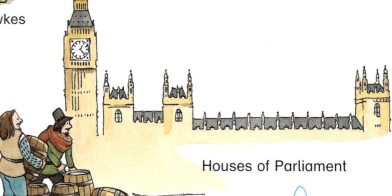

Houses of Parliament

gunpowder: Schießpulver
treason: Verrat
plot: Verschwörung

Remember, remember the Fifth of November,
gunpowder, treason and plot.
I see no reason why gunpowder treason,
should ever be forgot.

Look in the sky. See them fly.
Fireworks shooting up so high.
Red, yellow and green so bright.
Bang! Pop! Whizzzzz!
On Guy Fawkes night.

1 Listen and point.
2 Learn one of the rhymes by heart.

▶ Ich kann erzählen, wie Guy Fawkes Day heute gefeiert wird.

Guy Fawkes Day today

The 5th of November is a very special day for British children. It's also called Bonfire Night. The children buy fireworks with their parents.

In some cities there are parades with big Guy Fawkes figures. The 'Guy' is burnt in a big bonfire.

Everybody eats sweets, some children bake marshmallows and apples in the fire.
At night there are big firework displays.

1 Read the text. Find the pictures.
2 Talk about the text in German.

▶ Ich kann etwas über das erste Thanksgiving erzählen.

The first Thanksgiving

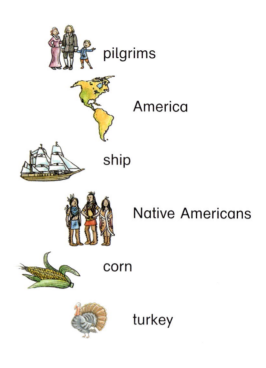

In 1620 about 100 sailed from England to on their called Mayflower. It was a hard trip to . They landed at Plymouth Rock in December 1620. The first winter was very cold. The helped to build houses. In spring they showed the how to plant , hunt and catch fish. In autumn the were very thankful and invited the to come to a big meal and eat . This was the first Thanksgiving.

1. Look at the pictures and the words. Then read the text.
2. Talk about the first Thanksgiving.
3. Do a role-play.

▶ Ich kann etwas über einen traditionellen amerikanischen Feiertag erzählen.

Thanksgiving today

A turkey is a funny bird.
His head goes wobble, wobble.
And all he says is just one word:
Gobble, gobble, gobble.

On the fourth Thursday in November people celebrate Thanksgiving.
It is the most important holiday in the USA. On this day families get together.
Sons, daughters, grandparents, uncles, aunts and cousins come home.
The traditional food is turkey, potatoes, pumpkin and corn.
Before dinner they say thank you for all the good things in their lives.
There is a big Thanksgiving parade in New York.
In the afternoon, most families watch American football on TV.

1 Read the text.

2 Talk about Thanksgiving today in German.

▶ Ich kann etwas über den Ursprung des St Patrick's Day erzählen.

St Patrick's Day

A leprechaun is small and green.
He hides where he cannot be seen.
But if you catch one on this very day,
He must give his gold away.

St Patrick's Day is on the 17th of March. On this day, Irish people all over the world remember St Patrick. He came to Ireland 1,500 years ago and talked to people about God. His symbol was a shamrock.

A leprechaun is a fairy.
He looks like a little man with a beard.
It brings good luck to find a leprechaun and his gold at the end of a rainbow.

1. Listen and read along.
2. Learn the rhyme by heart.
3. Talk about the poster.

▶ Ich kann erzählen, wie St Patrick's Day heute gefeiert wird.

St Patrick's Day today

On St Patrick's Day people wear green clothes and big hats, sometimes with shamrocks.

They eat green sweets and drink green drinks.

They have parades with music and dance groups.

In some towns, people dye the river green – like in Chicago.

1. Look at the pictures. Read the text.
2. Find out more about St Patrick's Day.

Landeskundliche Informationen über St-Patrick's-Day-Bräuche erhalten.

The story of the leprechaun

One night a man walked along a forest path. He heard the tap-tapping of a tiny hammer. This was a leprechaun mending shoes.

The man knew if he could catch the leprechaun he would learn where the little man had buried his pot of gold.

The man grabbed the leprechaun.

1 Listen to the story.
2 Read the story.
3 Do a role-play.

▶ Ich kann eine Geschichte verstehen.

The leprechaun showed the man
the bush where the pot of gold was buried.

The man had no spade to dig up the gold.
So he tied his red neckerchief to the bush
to find it again.

He made the leprechaun promise
not to take the neckerchief away.

He ran home to get a spade.

When he came back with his spade, the leprechaun was gone.
But there was a red neckerchief on every bush in the forest.

Fit for five

2

1

3

4

5

1 Play the game.

6

7

8

10

9

- 🎲 Give me five.
- 🎲 Ask a question.
- 🎲 Talk about the picture.
- 🎲 Do a role-play.
- 🎲 Make a riddle.
- 🎲 Take a card.

Superbrain

	People	Places	Activities
1	Who is John Silver? 100	Where does Ms Johnson work? 100	What does Jim want to do on Treasure Island? 100
2	Who is Mr Williams? 80	What can you visit at Baker Street 221b? 80	What do you do to protect your eyes? 80
3	Who is Cathy? 60	Where does Cathy live? 60	What does Lisa want to borrow in the library? 60
4	Who works with a tablet in the library? 40	Where can you watch the feeding of the seals? 40	What does a police woman do? 40
5	Who is Ms Li? 20	Where can you borrow books? 20	What do you do in ICT? 20
6	Who are Lisa's best friends? 10	Where did Lisa go in her holidays? 10	What do you do at school? 10
	People	Places	Activities

1 Answer the questions.
2 Think of more questions.

sixty-two   Inhalte dieses Buches wiederholen.

People	Places	Activities	
Who was St Patrick? 100	Where does Mr Miller work? 100	What do British children do on Bonfire night? 100	1
Who wins the Highland Games? 80	What did Guy Fawkes want to blow up? 80	What happens on Thanksgiving Day? 80	2
Who helps on Earth day to fill the glass bag? 60	Where do parrots originally live? 60	What do the children do on Earth day? 60	3
Who is 58 years old and brings letters? 40	Where can you go on holiday? 40	What does a zookeeper do? 40	4
Who lives in Canada and likes skiing? 20	Where do the children collect wrappings? 20	What can you do during Golden Time? 20	5
Who is from New York? 10	Where does Amy live? 10	What can you do in your holidays? 10	6
People	Places	Activities	

How to communicate

Ich spreche meinen Gesprächspartner direkt an und schaue ihn dabei an.

Ich versuche in ganzen Sätzen zu sprechen.

My favourite animal is an elephant.

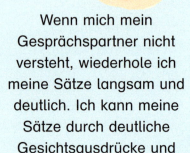

Wenn mich mein Gesprächspartner nicht versteht, wiederhole ich meine Sätze langsam und deutlich. Ich kann meine Sätze durch deutliche Gesichtsausdrücke und Gesten unterstützen.

Das hilft mir beim Sprechen.

Wenn ich etwas nicht verstehe, sage ich „Sorry, I don't understand". Wenn mein Gesprächspartner einen Satz nicht formulieren kann, versuche ich ihm zu helfen.

Wenn nötig, zeige ich auf Gegenstände oder Personen.

You have got a dog?

Wenn ich etwas beim ersten Mal nicht verstehe, sage ich „Can you say it again, please?"

Durch meine Betonung im Satz kann ich deutlich machen, dass ich etwas frage.

How to do a presentation

Ich schlage Wörter zu einem Thema in einem Wörterbuch nach und sammle sie.

Ich ordne Stichwörter in einer Mindmap.

My favourite sport is …

Ich überlege mir passende Sätze.

Beim Vortragen schaue ich meine Zuhörer an und versuche frei und deutlich zu sprechen.

Das hilft mir beim Erstellen einer Präsentation.

Ich suche Bilder aus und schreibe Stichwörter dazu auf.

Ich fertige ein Poster an.

Wenn mir ein Wort während der Präsentation nicht einfällt, stelle ich es pantomimisch dar oder zeige darauf, wenn es in meiner Nähe ist.

Wenn ich nicht weiß, wie ich ein Wort ausspreche, frage ich meine Mitschüler oder meine Lehrkraft.

Ich übe meinen Vortrag.

sixty-five

How to check my texts

How to work with notes

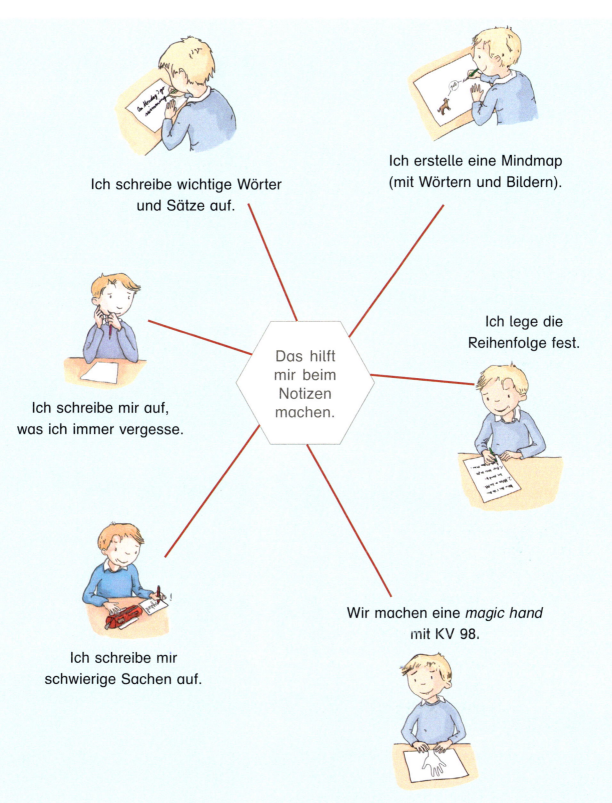

Graffiti

Step 1

Form groups. Choose a colour.

Step 2

Start at one table. Do the task together.

Step 3

Wait for the bell. Move to the next tables.

Step 5

Complete the posters.

Step 6

Go back to your poster. Talk about it.

1. Make a poster about your favourite pets.

Magic hand

1 Think
Think about a task. Use sheet 98.

2 Pair
Talk to your partner about your hand.

3 Share
Present your partner's hand to a group.

1 Make a magic hand about your favourite things.

Look it up

A

a/an	ein, eine, ein
a lot of …	viele
about	über
accident	der Unfall
age	das Alter
ape	der Menschenaffe
Art	der Kunstunterricht
assembly	die Schulversammlung
at	an/bei/in/um
Australia	Australien
autumn	der Herbst

B

back	zurück
baker	der Bäcker, die Bäckerin
balcony	der Balkon
ball	der Ball
banana	die Banane
bark	bellen
basket	der Korb
bathroom	das Badezimmer
be	sein
beach	der Strand
beak	der Schnabel
bear	der Bär
beautiful	wunderschön
because	weil
bed	das Bett
bedroom	das Schlafzimmer, auch: eigenes Zimmer
behind	hinter
bench	die Bank
big	groß
bike	das Fahrrad
bin	der Mülleimer
bird's eye-view	die Vogelperspektive
birthday	der Geburtstag
black	schwarz
blackboard	die (grüne) Tafel
blue	blau
board game	das Brettspiel
boat	das Boot
body part	der Körperteil
book	das Buch
bookshelf	das Bücherregal
borrow a book	ein Buch ausleihen
bottle	die Flasche
boy	der Junge
bread	das Brot
break	die Pause
breakfast	das Frühstück
bridge	die Brücke
British	britisch
broken	zerbrochen
brother	der Bruder
brown	braun
brush my teeth	meine Zähne putzen
bunk bed	das Stockbett
buried	hier: vergraben
busdriver	der Busfahrer
bush	der Busch
butler	der Butler
butter	die Butter
buy	kaufen
bye	tschüss

C

cake	der Kuchen, die Torte
call	(an)rufen
camel	das Kamel

camping site	der Campingplatz	colour	die Farbe, anmalen
can	die Dose	come	kommen
can/can't	können/nicht können	command	der Befehl
Canada	Kanada	compare	vergleichen
captain	der Kapitän	complete	vervollständigen
car mechanic	der Automechaniker/ die Automechanikerin	copy	die Kopie, kopieren, abschreiben
car	das Auto	corn	der Mais
caravan	der Wohnwagen	count	zählen
card	die Karte	country	das Land
carpet	der Teppich	cow	die Kuh
castle	das Schloss	Crafts	der Werkunterricht
cat	die Katze	crocodile	das Krokodil
catch	fangen	crown	die Krone
celebrate	feiern	cucumber	die Salatgurke
chair	der Stuhl	cup	die Tasse
chat	der Chat, das Gespräch	cupboard	der Schrank
cheese	der Käse	cut	schneiden
chicken	das Huhn		
child, children	das Kind, die Kinder		

D

chimpanzee	der Schimpanse
chips	die Pommes Frites
chocolate	die Schokolade
cinema	das Kino
circle	der Kreis, einkreisen
class	die Klasse
classmate	der/die Mitschüler/in
classroom	das Klassenzimmer
clock	die Uhr
climb	klettern
cloud	die Wolke
coconut	die Kokosnuss
coffee	der Kaffee
cold	kalt
collect waste	Müll sammeln
collect	sammeln

daily	täglich
dance	der Tanz, tanzen
danger	die Gefahr
dangerous	gefährlich
dark	dunkel
day	der Tag
dear	lieb, lieber, liebe
dentist	der Zahnarzt/die Zahnärztin
describe	beschreiben
desk	der Schreibtisch
detective	der Detektiv
dialogue	der Dialog
dice	der Würfel, die Würfel
dictionary	das Wörterbuch
different	unterschiedlich

seventy-one

dinner	die warme Mahlzeit	father	der Vater
dinosaur	der Dinosaurier	favourite	lieblings-
dirty	schmutzig	feather	die Feder
dive	tauchen	feed	füttern
doctor	der Arzt/die Ärztin	feeling	das Gefühl
dog	der Hund	ferry	die Fähre
door	die Tür	fight	der Kampf
down	hinunter, unten	find (out)	(heraus-)finden
draw	zeichnen	fine	gut
dream	der Traum	firefighter	der Feuerwehrmann
dress	das Kleid, anziehen	fireworks	das Feuerwerk
drink	das Getränk, trinken	first	erst
dye	färben	fish	der Fisch
		flag	die Flagge
		flat	die Wohnung
		floor	der Boden, hier: das Stockwerk

E

earth	die Erde
eat	essen
egg	das Ei
elephant	der Elefant
empty	leer
endangered	bedroht
enemy	der (Fress)Feind
England	England
English	Englisch
evening	der Abend
everybody	jeder, jede, jedes
explain	erklären

flower	die Blume
fly	die Fliege/fliegen
food	das Essen
football	der Fußball
forest	der Wald
freetime	die Freizeit
Friday	Freitag
friend	der Freund/die Freundin
from	von
fun	der Spaß, lustig
furniture	die Möbel

F

fairy	die Fee
fairy tale	das Märchen
false	falsch
family	die Familie
famous	berühmt
farmer	der Bauer
fast	schnell

G

game	das Spiel
garbage	der Müll
gate	das Tor
German	Deutsch
Germany	Deutschland

get dressed	sich anziehen
get up	aufstehen
ghost	das Gespenst
giraffe	die Giraffe
girl	das Mädchen
give	geben
glass	das Glas
glue	kleben, der Klebstoff
go	gehen
go fishing	angeln (gehen)
go hiking	wandern (gehen)
Golden Time	die Freiarbeitszeit
good	gut
goodbye	auf Wiedersehen
grandparents	die Großeltern
great	toll, super
Great Britain	Großbritannien
green	grün
grey	grau
group	die Gruppe
guess	raten

H

habitat	der Lebensraum
hair	das Haar, die Haare
hairdresser	der Frisör/die Frisörin
hall	die Diele
hamster	der Hamster
hand	die Hand
happy	glücklich, froh
have breakfast	frühstücken
have dinner	(zu) Abend essen / die Hauptmahlzeit einnehmen
have lunch	(zu) Mittag essen
he	er
head	der Kopf
headmaster, headmistress	der Rektor/die Rektorin
headphone	die Kopfhörer
hear	hören
hedge	die Hecke
hedgehog	der Igel
hello	hallo
help	die Hilfe, helfen
her	ihr (wie in *ihr* Kleid)
here	hier
Here you are.	Bitteschön.
high	hoch
hike	wandern / die Wanderung
hippo	das Nilpferd
his	sein (wie in *sein* Buch)
hobby	das Hobby
holiday	der Feiertag, der Urlaub
homework	die Hausaufgaben
hoof, hooves	der Huf, die Hufe
horn	das Horn
horse	das Pferd
hot	heiß
hot chocolate	die heiße Schokolade
house	das Haus
how	wie
hungry	hungrig

I

I	ich
I'd / I would	ich würde
I'm / I am	ich bin
I've / I have	ich habe
ice cream	die Eiscreme
ICT	der Informatikunterricht

seventy-three **73**

in front of	vor	lemonade	die Limonade
in	in	leopard	der Leopard
India	Indien	leprechaun	der Kobold
instruction	die Anweisung	letter	der Brief
instrument	das (Musik)instrument	lifeguard	der/die Rettungsschwimmer/in
interest	das Interesse	like	1. mögen 2. wie
invitation	die Einladung	line	die Zeile, die Strophe
invite	einladen	lion	der Löwe
Ireland	Irland	list	die Liste, auflisten
is	ist	listen	zuhören
island	die Insel	little	klein
it	es	live	leben
		living room	das Wohnzimmer
		long	lang
		look	schauen, sehen
		look up	nachschlagen
		lose	verlieren
		loud	laut
		lunch	das Mittagessen

J

jam	die Marmelade
jeans	die Jeans
juice	der Saft
jump	springen

K

keyword	das Schlüsselwort
kill	töten
kindergarten teacher	der Kindergärtner/die Kindergärtnerin
king	der König
kitchen	die Küche
knight	der Ritter
know	wissen

L

label	beschriften
lake	der See
lamp	die Lampe
language	die Sprache
left	links

M

magic	die Magie, magisch
make	machen, tun
man	der Mann
mane	die Mähne
many	viele
map	die Karte
mark	markieren
market	der Markt
match	verbinden
Maths	der Mathematikunterricht
me	mich
meal	das Mahl
media room	der Medienraum

meet	treffen
mend	hier: flicken
menu	die Speisekarte
miss (a turn)	1. aussetzen 2. etwas vermissen
missing	fehlend
Monday	Montag
money	das Geld
monkey	der Affe
month	der Monat
moon	der Mond
more	mehr
morning	der Morgen
most	meist, höchst
mother	die Mutter
motor bike	das Motorrad
mountain	der Berg
mouse	die Maus
move	bewegen
much	viel
Music	der Musikunterricht
my	mein, meine, mein

N

name	der Name, benennen
nature	die Natur
Native Americans	die Ureinwohner Amerikas
neckerchief	das Halstuch
need	brauchen
new	neu
newspaper	die Zeitung
next	als Nächstes, das Nächste
next to	neben
nice	schön
no	nein
nobody	niemand, keiner
noisy	laut
not	nicht
notebook	das Notizbuch
nothing	nichts
now	jetzt, nun
number	die Zahl, nummerieren
nurse	die Krankenschwester / der Krankenpfleger

O

o'clock	(acht) Uhr
office worker	der Sachbearbeiter / die Sachbearbeiterin
okay / OK	okay
old	alt
on	auf, im
orange	1. die Orange 2. orange
other	andere
our	unser, unsere, unser
out	raus
own	eigener, eigenes, eigene

P

paint	malen
pair	1. das Paar 2. paaren
palace	der Palast
parcel	das Paket
parents	die Eltern
parrot	der Papagei
part	der Teil
party	die Feier
paw	die Pfote
PE	der Sportunterricht

seventy-five 75

pen	der Füller
pencil	der Bleistift
penguin	der Pinguin
pen pal	der Brieffreund, die Brieffreundin
pet	1. das Haustier 2. streicheln
phone	1. das Telefon 2. telefonieren
pick up	aufheben
picnic	das Picknick
picture	das Bild
piece	das Stück
pilgrim	der Pilger / die Pilgerin
pilot	der Pilot / die Pilotin
pink	pink
piping	das Dudelsackspielen
pirate	der Pirat
plan	planen
plane	das Flugzeug
plastic	das Plastik
play	spielen
please	bitte
plum	die Pflaume
pocket	die (Hosen-)Tasche
pocket money	das Taschengeld
poem	das Gedicht
point	zeigen
polar bear	der Eisbär
police woman	die Polizistin
pound	das Pfund
practise	üben
present	1. präsentieren 2. das Geschenk
preposition	die Präposition
presentation	die Präsentation
price	der Preis
prince	der Prinz
princess	die Prinzessin
promise	versprechen / das Versprechen
proud	stolz
pullover	der Pullover
put	legen, setzen, stellen
putting the stone	Steinweitwurf

Q

queen	die Königin
question	die Frage

R

rabbit	der Hase, das Kaninchen
racing car	das Rennauto
read	lesen
red	rot
remember	sich erinnern
repeat	wiederholen
rescue	retten
rhino	das Nashorn
rhyme	der Reim
ride	fahren, reiten
right	1. rechts 2. richtig
ring	der Ring
river	der Fluss
roar	brüllen
role-play	das Rollenspiel
roll the dice	würfeln
room	das Zimmer
rope bridge	die Hängebrücke
rubber	der Radierer

ruler	das Lineal
run	rennen, laufen

S

sad	traurig
safe	sicher
sail	segeln
salad	der Salat
Saturday	Samstag
say	sagen
scared	ängstlich
school	die Schule
schoolbag	der Schulranzen
Science	der Sachunterricht
scoop	die Kugel (Eis)
Scotland	Schottland
sea	das Meer
seaside	die Küste
season	die Jahreszeit
see	sehen
sentence	der Satz
shamrock	das Kleeblatt
share	teilen
she	sie (wie in: *sie* hat)
ship	das Schiff
shirt	das Hemd
shoes	die Schuhe
shop	1. der Laden
	2. einkaufen
shop assistant	der Verkäufer / die Verkäuferin
show	zeigen
sight	die Sehenswürdigkeit
sing	singen
sister	die Schwester
sit down	hinsetzen
skateboard	das Skateboard
skirt	der Rock
sleep	schlafen
slow	langsam
small	klein
snake	die Schlange
sofa	das Sofa
some	etwas
sorry	Entschuldigung
soup	die Suppe
South Africa	Südafrika
spade	der Spaten
speak	sprechen
special	besonders
spin	drehen
sports	die Sportart
spring	der Frühling
squirrel	das Eichhörnchen
stand (up)	(auf-)stehen
stay at home	zuhause bleiben
story	die Geschichte
strawberry	die Erdbeere
strong	stark
subject	das Unterrichtsfach
suddenly	plötzlich
summer	der Sommer
sun	die Sonne
Sunday	Sonntag
survey	die Umfrage
sweets	die Süßigkeiten
swim	schwimmen

T

tablet	das Tablet
tail	der Schwanz
take (out)	(heraus-)nehmen

seventy-seven

talk	sprechen
task	die Aufgabe
tea	der Tee
teacher	der Lehrer/die Lehrerin
tell	erzählen, sagen
tennis	Tennis
text message	die Textnachricht
thank you/thanks	danke
Thanksgiving	das Thanksgivingfest
the	der, die, das
then	dann
there	da
they	sie (wie in *sie* sind)
think	denken, überlegen
this	dies
through	durch
Thursday	Donnerstag
tick	ankreuzen (mit Häkchen)
tidy up	aufräumen
tiger	der Tiger
time	die Zeit
timetable	der Stundenplan
tiny	winzig
tip	der Tipp
tired	müde
to	bis, nach, zu
toilet	die Toilette
tomato	die Tomate
tonight	heute Abend/Nacht
tooth, teeth	der Zahn, die Zähne
tortoise	die Landschildkröte
tossing the caber	Baumstammweitwurf
tower	der Turm
toy	das Spielzeug
train	der Zug
treasure	der Schatz
tree	der Baum
tricky	schwierig
trouble	die Schwierigkeit
trunk	der (Elefanten-)Rüssel
Tuesday	Dienstag
turkey	der Truthahn
turtle	die Wasserschildkröte

U

under	unter
underground	die Untergrundbahn
United States of America	Vereinigte Staaten von Amerika
up	hinauf
us	uns
use	benutzen

V

vampire	der Vampir
vegetable	das Gemüse
very	sehr
vet	der Tierarzt/die Tierärztin
visit	besuchen

W

waiter, waitress	der Kellner/die Kellnerin
walk	laufen, (spazieren) gehen
wardrobe	der Kleiderschrank
warning	die Warnung
watch (TV)	(fern-)sehen
water	das Wasser, wässern
way	der Weg

we	wir
Wednesday	Mittwoch
week	die Woche
weekday	der Wochentag
weekend	das Wochenende
welcome	willkommen
what	was
What a pity!	Wie schade!
when	wann
where	wo
white	weiß
who	wer
whole	ganz
window	das Fenster
winter	der Winter
wish	der Wunsch / wünschen
with	mit
word	das Wort
work	arbeiten
world	die Welt
wrapping / wrapper	die Verpackung
write (down)	(auf-)schreiben
wrong	falsch

Y

year	das Jahr
yellow	gelb
yes	ja
you	du
your	1. dein, deine, dein
	2. euer, eure, euer

Z

zebra	das Zebra
zoo	der Zoo
zookeeper	der Tierpfleger

Textbook für Englisch in Klasse 4

Abbildungsnachweis:
Titel: Titel: iStockphoto.com, Calgary (ilbusca)
3.1: Matthias Muth, Biederitz; 3.2-3: mauritius images GmbH, Mittenwald (beide Loop Images/Eric Nathan); 3.4 (Thompson), 3.5 (jan zandee): Colourbox.com, Odense; 6.1: alamy images, Abingdon/Oxfordshire (Jeff Morgan 15); 11.1: Colourbox.com, Odense; 11.2: mauritius images GmbH, Mittenwald (Kellerman/Alamy); 11.3-4 (Nicolino): Colourbox.com, Odense; 11.5: fotolia.com, New York (emiliano85); 17.1: alamy images, Abingdon/Oxfordshire (Whiting & Associates); 22.1 (age/Rupeta), 22.2 (Stockbroker), 22.3 (United Archives), 22.4 (United Archives), 24.1 (Levenson/Alamy), 24.2 (Atkin/Alamy), 24.3 (Levenson/Alamy), 24.4 (White/Alamy), 24.5 (Ryall/Alamy): mauritius images GmbH, Mittenwald; 25.1: alamy images, Abingdon/Oxfordshire (Greg Balfour Evans); 25.2 (NAN), 25.3 (Studio Porto Sabbia), 25.4 (simonidadj), 25.5 (gradt): fotolia.com, New York; 29.1: alamy images, Abingdon/Oxfordshire (Mega), 29.2: Shutterstock.com, New York (Kamira); 29.3: alamy images, Abingdon/Oxfordshire (Jordan); 36.1-3: iStockphoto.com, Calgary (alle Steward); 37.1: alamy images, Abingdon/Oxfordshire (Tripplaar); 38.1: mauritius images GmbH, Mittenwald (Lumi Images/Pupeter-Secen); 38.2 (rcfotostock), 38.3 (somartin): fotolia.com, New York; 38.4: Getty Images, München (Radius Images); 38.5: fotolia.com, New York (Kosmider); 38.6 (visual7), 38.7 (Locke): iStockphoto.com, Calgary; 38.8: fotolia.com, New York (lucamedei); 38.9 (Anthony Baggett), 38.10 (Contributor), 38.11 (Heger), 8.12 (visual7): iStockphoto.com, Calgary; 39 Hintergrund: fotolia.com, New York (Spencer); 39.1: Getty Images, München (Rubberball); 39.2: fotolia.com, New York (OHRAUGE); 39.3: iStockphoto.com, Calgary (Davoust); 39.4: Getty Images, München (Kemp/Rubberball); 39.5 (Moller), 39.6 (visual7): iStockphoto.com, Calgary; 39.7: Getty Images, München (Ocean); 39.8: iStockphoto.com, Calgary (visual7); 39.9: fotolia.com, New York (Hackemann); 40.1: mauritius images GmbH, Mittenwald (Loop Images); 40.2: fotolia.com, New York (Shepulova), 40.3: mauritius images GmbH, Mittenwald (Frei); 41.1 (Hopkins), 41.2 (ilse schrama): alamy images, Abingdon/Oxfordshire; 41.3: mauritius images GmbH, Mittenwald (World Pictures); 41.4: alamy images, Abingdon/Oxfordshire (schrama); 42.1-3: Michaela Schönau, Stuttgart; 42.4: Anna Van Montagu, Ahaus; 42.5: Michaela Schönau, Stuttgart; 48.1: action press, Hamburg; 48.2: Shutterstock.com, New York (Dutourdumonde Photography); 48.3: iStockphoto.com, Calgary (Matt84); 48.4: mauritius images GmbH, Mittenwald (AGE); 48.5: iStockphoto.com, Calgary (riki76); 53.1: fotolia.com, New York (Bikeworldtravel); 53.2: Gisela Ehlers, Hüttenwohld; 53.3 (GRANT ROONEY PREMIUM/Alamy), 53.4 (Smith/Alamy): mauritius images GmbH, Mittenwald; 55.1: iStockphoto.com, Calgary (fstop123); 55.2: Reuters, Berlin (Tapleton); 55.3: Caro Fotoagentur GmbH, Berlin (Oberhaeuser); 57.1 (Vidler), 57.2 (foodcollection), 57.3 (foodcollection): mauritius images GmbH, Mittenwald; 57.4: fotolia.com, New York (dream79); 57.5 (imageBROKER/Kazmaier), 57.6 (age/Fox): mauritius images GmbH, Mittenwald.
Alle übrigen Fotos: Andreas Tauber, Berlin

Musik- und Textnachweis
S. 25: Song: With my own two hands: Text/Musik: Ben C. Harper. © BMG Gold Songs BMG Rights Management GmbH, Berlin. Alle anderen Songtexte: Gisela Ehlers, Grit Kahstein, Matthias Muth und Hannelore Tait. S. 47: Song: Coconut cream rap: Text: nach Frank Leto.

westermann GRUPPE

© 2017 Bildungshaus Schulbuchverlage
Westermann Schroedel Diesterweg Schöningh Winklers GmbH Braunschweig
www.schroedel.de
Das Werk und seine Teile sind urheberrechtlich geschützt. Jede Nutzung in anderen als den gesetzlich zugelassenen Fällen bedarf der vorherigen schriftlichen Einwilligung des Verlages. Hinweis zu § 52 a UrhG: Weder das Werk noch seine Teile dürfen ohne Einwilligung gescannt und in ein Netzwerk eingestellt werden. Dies gilt auch für Intranets von Schulen und sonstigen Bildungseinrichtungen.
Druck A1 / Jahr 2017
Alle Drucke der Serie A sind inhaltlich unverändert.

Redaktion: Stephanie Manz
Herstellung: Katja Schumann
Umschlaggestaltung: Visuelle Lebensfreude, mit einer Illustration von Angela Glökler
Satz und technische Umsetzung: Druck- und Medienhaus Sigert GmbH, Braunschweig
Druck und Bindung: westermann druck GmbH
ISBN 978-3-507-02854-8